CON

Map references are denoted in the text by ❶ Greater Edinburgh
❷ Central Edinburgh ❸ Glasgow and ❹ Edinburgh region

edinburgh places to see

Edinburgh is a great city for sightseeing. Not only can you cover the vast majority of its sights on foot, but while you are actually getting from A to B, the city is a sight in itself that constantly unfolds before you; the magnificent green swathe of Princes Street Gardens topped by the omnipresent castle; the film-set-like medieval passageways leading up to and off the Royal Mile; the glorious Georgian terraces of the New Town and the spectacular verdant countryside of Holyrood Park. And there's probably no other city in the world with so many bridges and hills offering lots of unusual and spectacular viewpoints. Edinburgh's museums and galleries are world-class and its very fabric oozes history, but it has also invested wisely in the future with major attractions such as Our Dynamic Earth and the Royal Yacht *Britannia*.

see it places to see

Royal Mile & the Old Town

Edinburgh Castle ❷ 5B

Symbol of the city and a magnet for the eye from all over the Old Town, a royal residence has stood on this brooding volcanic crag for nearly a thousand years. The oldest surviving part is St Margaret's Chapel, c. 1100, though the castle began to assume its present shape around the mid-16th century. The old palace part houses Scotland's splendid crown jewels, 'The Honours of Scotland', while reminders of battles

Edinburgh Castle from Princes Street Gardens

past include the monstrous Mons Meg cannon and the Vaults where prisoners were held. Time your visit to experience the near-deafening explosion of the One O'Clock Gun, fired daily except Sundays, originally as a time signal to shipping.
Open Apr-Oct 9.30am-6pm, Nov-Mar 9.30am-5pm. Last tickets 45 min before closing. Adm. Castlehill, T: 0131 225 9846, www.edinburghcastle.gov.uk

Gladstone's Land ❷ 5D

If you want to know how a wealthy merchant's house appeared in early 17th-century Edinburgh, step inside this atmospherically preserved six-storey tenement. The ground floor was let as a shop while the Gledstane family and lessees of various social standings resided in painted and panelled upstairs chambers.
Open Apr-Oct Mon-Sat 10am-5pm, Sun 2-5pm. Adm. Lawnmarket, T: 0844 493 2120, www.nts.org.uk

St Giles' Cathedral ❷ 5D

Almost as mighty a presence as the castle, grimy grey St Giles'

Cathedral – and particularly its late-15th-century open crown spire – is one of Edinburgh's best-known landmarks. The High Kirk, as it is known, was rebuilt over the

The Heart of the City

Outside St Giles' Cathedral and set into the pavement is a heart-shaped pattern of stone blocks. This is the Heart of Midlothian, named after Sir Walter Scott's eponymous novel. It marks the site of the old tollbooth that stood here for some 400 years until 1817. Deacon Brodie (see box, p.5) was held prisoner here. Don't be surprised to see the locals spitting upon it – it supposedly brings good luck!

St Giles' Cathedral

100 years following a fire in 1385, though subsequent alterations have all but effaced its medieval character. Here preacher John Knox (*see p.6*) launched the Scottish Reformation and his statue stands in the nave. Look out for memorials to Robert Louis Stevenson (a bronze relief) and Robert Burns (the enigmatic modern west window). Note too the carvings of the stalls, canopies and bosses, and the flamboyant Neo-Gothic Thistle Chapel, exquisitely crafted between 1909-11. *Open May-Sept,*

Mon-Fri 9am-7pm, Sat 9am-5pm, Sun 1pm-5pm; Oct-Apr 9am-5pm. Royal Mile, T: 0131 255 9442, www.stgilescathedral.org.uk

The Real Mary King's Close ❷ 5D

Opened to the public to much acclaim, Mary King's Close is the eponymous main street of a warren of narrow alleyways (or closes) which, between the 16th and 19th centuries, surrounded Old Town tenements (apartment blocks) up to seven storeys high. In 1753 the Burgh authorities demolished the upper tenement floors and built the Royal Exchange (now the City Chambers) over the top of the lower floors, leaving a maze of subterranean houses below. Guides take you on a tour of these forgotten rooms with tableaux and sound and light effects to interpret the squalid conditions of life at this time, complete with the plague and, inevitably, a ghost or two. *Open Apr-Oct 10am-10pm, Nov-Mar 10am-4pm (last tickets one hour before closing). Min age five. Adm. 2 Warriston's Close, T: 0845 0706 244, www.realmarykingsclose.com*

Deacon Brodie

William Brodie was, by day, a highly respected Edinburgh town councillor, cabinetmaker and deacon (president) of the guild of Wrights and Masons. By night, however, he gambled and womanised. To pay off his debts, he became a robber and is thought to be the inspiration for Robert Louis Stevenson's famous novel *Jekyll and Hyde.* Brodie was caught and hanged in 1788 on a gallows that, supposedly, he had crafted himself. You can tread in his footsteps in The Deacon's House in Brodie Close, opposite the Deacon Brodie pub on the Royal Mile. Now a pleasant café, it once belonged to the Brodie family.

Ghosts & Ghoulies

In medieval times Edinburgh was a terrible place to live, with horrendously insanitary conditions (*see box, p.10*), the plague, religious intolerance, witch-hunting and summary executions all part of everyday life. To relive this dark past, take a tour through the snaking dark wynds, closes and subterranean vaults of the Old Town, and be regaled with ghost stories (*see p.55*). The 'City of Dead' tour visits Greyfriars Kirkyard (*see p.12*) by night to relate the story of various poltergeists. *8.30pm, 9.15pm, 10pm nightly. Adm. T: 0131 225 9044, www.blackhart.uk.com*

John Knox House ❷ 5F

Right in the middle of the Royal Mile this charming four-storey house is probably the finest surviving 15th-century property in Scotland. Its association with Knox, the religious firebrand who led the Scottish Protestant Reformation, is tenuous – he may have died here in 1572 – but its interpretation of this period and what could be a dry subject is first class. The 'taped conversation' between Knox and Mary Queen of Scots, re-enacted from authentic sources, which plays on the upper floors, is both atmospheric and enlightening. *Open Mon-Sat 10am-5pm, Jul & Aug also Sun 12 noon-6pm. 43-45 High Street, T: 0131 556 9579, www.scottishstorytellingcentre.co.uk*

Museum of Childhood ❷ 5E

If you want to get all misty-eyed about the things you played with as a child, and see too what your parents and even grandparents made do with, then this wonderful collection will roll back the years. More poignant even than the vast collection of slightly sinister Victorian dolls and toys dating from the early 20th century is the very early, flickering and grainy black-and-white film of Edinburgh children playing long-forgotten traditional street games. *Open Mon-Sat 10am-5pm; Jul & Aug also Sun 12 noon-5pm. 42 High Street, T: 0131 529 4142, www.edinburghmuseums.org.uk*

The Museum of Edinburgh & The People's Story ❷ 5G

The first museum tells you everything you want to know about the city's history, from its seventh-century origins as Dun Edin, entertainingly displayed in a warren-like 16th-century house. Just across the street, the excellent People's Story adds a human element with case stories and simulated living and working conditions of ordinary Edinburgh folk from the 18th-century to the present day. *Both open Mon-Sat 10am-5pm; Aug also Sun 12 noon-5pm, www.cac. org.uk* **The Museum of Edinburgh:** *142 Canongate, T: 0131 529 4143,* **People's Story:** *163 Canongate*

Tollbooth, T: 0131 529 4057.
www.edinburghmuseums.org.uk

Holyrood

Palace of Holyroodhouse ❷ 5H

The origins of the palace can be traced in the romantic ruins of the adjacent Holyrood Abbey, whose guesthouse was used by early

Imposing façade of the Palace of Holyroodhouse

Scottish kings, when in Edinburgh, in preference to the cold and draughty castle. King James IV built the first proper palace around 1500 but today's building is a 1671 design by William Bruce. Tours take in Mary Queen of Scots' bed chamber, the elaborate State Apartments, and the Great Gallery commissioned by Charles II, where all preceding 110

Scottish kings are Stuart lookalikes! Holyroodhouse is one of the Queen's official residences in Scotland and at certain times (usually mid May and first week June to first week July) may be closed to the public. In the Queen's Gallery there may be seven-10 days closure between exhibitions.
Open Nov-Mar (guided tour obligatory) 9.30am-4.30pm, Apr-Oct

Mary Queen of Scots
Born at Linlithgow Palace (❹) in 1542, Mary spent her life in a web of intrigue. In 1566, her husband Lord Darnley murdered Mary's secretary David Rizzio at Holyrood (*see left*), and she asked the Earl of Bothwell to kill Darnley. When this came to light, she abdicated and threw herself at the mercy of her English cousin, Elizabeth I, who promptly imprisoned her. Mary was implicated in a plot to overthrow Elizabeth and was beheaded in 1587.

A Home for Scottish Parliament ❷ 5H

The most controversial building in Scottish history was finally completed in October 2004, ten times over budget and a cool three years past its original deadline. Its futuristic design, by Spanish architect Enric Miralles, initially divided opinion sharply, but it has won several major awards now that the shock waves have subsided. Everything is beautifully explained at the *Parliament Building Information Centre*, T: 0131 348 5000, www.scottish.parliament.uk

9.30am-6pm (last adm 1 hr before closing). Adm. Canongate, Royal Mile, T: 0131 556 5100, www.royalcollection.org.uk

Our Dynamic Earth ❷ 6H

This multi-media trip from the Big Bang to the present day was Edinburgh's major Millennium project and has been a big hit with visitors and critics alike. An elevator ride takes you back some 15 billion years where stars collide and planets are born around you. It's then a gallop through the ages, witnessing various life forms, biomes, geological phenomena and including lots of hands-on experiences – you even get to touch a real iceberg. Excellent family 'edu-tainmen'. *Open Apr-Aug daily 10am-6pm, Sept-Oct daily 10am-5pm, Nov-Mar Wed-Sun 10am-5pm (last adm 90mins before closing). Adm. Holyrood Road, T: 0131 550 7800, www.dynamicearth.co.uk*

Arthur's Seat & Holyrood Park ❷ 5H

Arthur's Seat, an enormous volcanic plug in the middle of Holyrood Park, is the city's highest point, at 823 ft (251 m). The 360-degree panorama from here stretching back to the Old Town and across Leith and the Forth is unbeatable. However, for the classic picture-postcard vista of Edinburgh Old Town, stand on top of Salisbury Crags, the rocky ridge that runs around Arthur's Seat and overlooks the palace (see p.7). Beware – it's always windy on top of Arthur's Seat but this is a must – a true highlight of any Edinburgh visit.

The volcanic plug of Arthur's Seat in the snow

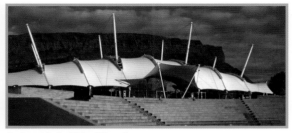

Our Dynamic Earth – Edinburgh's innovative museum

New Town

Calton Hill ❷ 3G

The views from Calton Hill, a mere 10-minute walk from Princes Street, are arguably the best in town. You'll also find here an eclectic collection of Classical-style monuments erected in the early 19th century, which led to Edinburgh being nicknamed 'the Athens of the North'. Most Athenian of all is the unfinished Parthenon-like National Monument, a memorial to the dead of the Napoleonic Wars. Adjacent is the 106-ft (32-m) tall Nelson Monument, an inverted telescope-shaped tower, dedicated to the great sealord. Climb its 143 steps for a spectacular 360-degree panorama. Other landmarks are the much-photographed Dugald Stewart Memorial, a circular pillared monument with a cupola, dedicated to a (now-forgotten) university professor, and the similarly grandiose Robert Burns Monument. *Nelson Monument open Apr-Sept, Mon 1pm-6pm, Tue-Sat 10am-6pm; Oct-Mar, Mon-Sat 10am-3pm. Adm. T: 0131 556 2716, www.edinburghmuseums.org.uk*

The Edinburgh Dungeon ❷ 5D

The dark side of Scottish and Edinburgh history, portrayed with gruesome gory glee in all-too-realistic tableaux and by scare-you-to-death actors. Meet Sawney Beane, the Leith cannibal; Burke & Hare; Deacon Brodie (*see box, p.5*) and experience bloody clan warfare. Not for the squeamish or young children, but teens love it. *Open Mon-Fri 11am-4pm, Sat-Sun 10.30am-4.30pm. Adm. Market Street, T: 0131 240 1001, www.thedungeons.com*

The National Monument at Calton Hill

Don't Swim in Nor' Loch

As beautiful as Princes Street Gardens are today, they have a very grimy past. Hollowed out by glacial action millions of years ago, the dip was filled with water to become a lake known as Nor' (north) Loch. The Old Town grew unchecked above the loch with no basic sanitation and all its filth and sewerage drained straight into the loch; dead animals and executed criminals were also added to the soup. Despite this, it provided much of the city's drinking water until the 1760s, when it was drained and the gardens laid out.

Princes Street Gardens ❷ 4B

The most glorious city gardens in Europe, if not the world, roll down from below the castle, run the length of Princes Street and play host to visitors and locals alike. In summer they are a riot of colour, and there is a splendid floral clock. In December and January an ice rink and giant ferris wheel are set up and the fair comes to town along with a German Christmas market. *See box, left.*

National Gallery of Scotland & Royal Scottish Academy ❷ 4D

The National Gallery is one of Britain's most enjoyable medium-sized galleries, exhibiting a collection of European and Scottish Art c.1300-1900. Most of the famous Old Masters from the 16th to 18th centuries have outstanding works here and the Impressionist collection features instantly recognisable canvasses by Monet, Degas and van Gogh. The highlight of the Scottish collection is Raeburn's wonderful *Reverend Robert Walker Skating on Duddingston Loch.* The adjacent Royal Scottish Academy stages acclaimed exhibitions and connects to the Galleries by way of the Weston Link which provides more exhibition space and a striking café-restaurant that

The Georgian elegance of Charlotte Square in the New Town

The Reverend Walker *in the National Gallery*

overlooks Princes Street Gardens. *Both open daily 10am-5pm, Thu 10am-7pm. Free. The Mound, T: 0131 624 6200, www.nationalgalleries.org*

Scott Monument ❷ 2D

This 200-ft (61-m) tall Gothic-pinnacled soot-blackened stone sky rocket is Edinburgh's most recognisable symbol. It was erected in 1846 by George Meikle Kemp in homage to Sir Walter Scott, the city's most loved (if sentimental) writer, and features 64 characters invented by him carved into the stones. Climb almost to the very top for great views over the city. *Open Apr-Sep Mon-Sat 9am-6pm, Sun 10am-6pm; Oct-Mar Mon-Sat 9am-3pm, Sun 10am-3pm. Adm. East Princes Street Gardens, T: 0131 529 4068, www.edinburghmuseums.org.uk*

Scottish National Portrait Gallery ❷ 3E

An excellent collection where you can put a face to famous historical names and see some modern interpretations of contemporary Scots such as Sean Connery and Robbie Coltrane. It's worth a visit too for the glittering mosaic frieze in its grand entrance hall, and its café (*see p.44*). The gallery is currently closed but will open in Autumn 2011. *Open daily 10am-5pm, Thur 10am-7pm. 1 Queen Street, T: 0131 624 6200, www.nationalgalleries.org*

Charlotte Square ❷ 3A

Charlotte Square is the finest Georgian ensemble in the New

Scott Monument

Town. Why else would Scotland's First Minister reside here? A few doors away at No. 7 is The Georgian House, where the National Trust for Scotland show you period life, upstairs and downstairs. On the opposite side of the square at No. 28 Charlotte Square, the NTS are custodians of another exquisite example of the Georgian age, complete with a gallery of modern

Scottish art and a cafe/restaurant (*see p.45*). **No. 28 Gallery & shop:** *open Mon-Fri 11am-3pm, Sun 12 noon-5pm;* **Café:** *open Mon-Sat 10am-5pm.* T: 0131 243 9300, www.nts.org.uk. **The Georgian House:** *open daily Apr-Oct 10am-5pm, Nov-24 Dec & Mar 11am-3pm. Adm. T: 0844 493 2118, www.nts.org.uk*

South of the City

Greyfriars Kirkyard ❷ 6D

They say Edinburgh's most famous graveyard is the last resting place for up to 325,000 souls, the majority unnamed, uncommemorated plague victims. What is for sure is that the memorial stones here – many 17th-century, in classic Hammer Horror Gothic style – are unequalled. It's eerie by day but if you're brave enough to explore after dark take a tour with City of the Dead (*see box, p.6*). Ironically the most famous grave here belongs to a dog, Greyfriars Bobby, whose tale is the only heartwarming thing to come from this chilling place (*see right*). www.greyfriarskirk.com

The little statue of Greyfriars Bobby

Greyfriars Bobby ❷ 6D

Bobby, a Skye terrier, belonged to an Edinburgh policemen, Jock Gray, who was buried in Greyfriars Kirkyard in 1858. Loyal to the last, Bobby refused to leave his side and kept a constant vigil by his master's grave. He was adopted by the locals, became an Edinbugh folk hero, and when he died 14 years later, special dispensation was given for Bobby to be buried alongside Jock. You'll find them both at the front of the churchyard. Just outside is Bobby's statue, opposite the Greyfriars Bobby pub. There's even been a Disney film about the 'wee dug'.

Royal Museum & Museum of Scotland (MoS) ❷ 6D

Occupying a striking sandstone-coloured modern interpretation of a baronial castle, the Museum of Scotland opened in 1998 as an extension to the Royal Museum. The latter is set around a three-storey Victorian hall of glass and iron, while the MoS is totally new wave. Both are very enjoyable and can easily occupy a couple of wet days. Don't try to rush it all in one go. The MoS deals with the history of Scotland; notable exhibits include the Lewis Chessmen and Mary Queen of Scots' jewellery. The Royal has a worldwide brief but is currently shut to the public until 2011 while

Palm House at the Royal Botanic Garden

The modernistic Museum of Scotland

it undergoes extensive renovation following a £46.4 million initiative to renew and reinvent the site. *Open daily 10am-5pm. Chambers Street, T: 0131 225 7534, www.nms.ac.uk*

Out of Town

The Royal Yacht Britannia ❶ 1F

After 44 years and over a million miles of royal globetrotting, the *Britannia* finally came to rest in Leith in 1997 and has been a huge draw for visitors ever since. It provides a fascinating insight into the royal lifestyle, more than any conventional palace could convey, helped along with an entertaining audio guide and a refreshingly unstuffy approach

to the subject. *Open Apr-Sept 9.30am-6pm, Oct-Mar 10am-3.30pm (last adm 90 mins before closing). It is advisable to pre-book in August. Adm. Ocean Terminal, Leith, T: 0131 555 5566, www.royalyachtbritannia.co.uk*

Scottish National Gallery of Modern Art & Dean Gallery ❶ 3D

If you enjoy bright and breezy modern art (no unmade beds or carved up cows here) you'll like both of these very accessible and attractive galleries, which stand opposite each other on the outskirts of the centre of town. The SNGMA is the larger, with 20th- and 21st-century works by Scottish artists and international superstars such as Picasso, Matisse, Warhol and Roy Lichtenstein. The Dean Gallery is dominated by Edinburgh-born sculptor Eduardo Paolozzi. However there are also important Dada and Surrealist works here by such luminaries as Magritte, Miró and Dalí. Both galleries have excellent cafés. **Both:** *open daily 10am-5pm, Thur 10am-7pm. Belford Road,*

T: 0131 624 2000, www.nationalgalleries.org

Royal Botanic Garden ❶ 2D

The 'Botanics' began life in 1670, as a research garden next to palatial Holyroodhouse (*see p.7*). It has long since exceeded this brief, moved to the suburbs and is now a favourite locals' and visitors' park, with some 72 acres of lovely walks. In April and May the rhododendrons are a picture. At any time the Glasshouse Experience, a complex of 10 linked greenhouses, including the 70-ft (21-m) high Palm House, is the highlight of a visit, transporting you through tropical, temperate and arid climes. The garden's Terrace Cafe enjoys a wonderful

The Royal Yacht Britannia *at Ocean Terminal*

Pair of Lemurs at Edinburgh Zoo

view of the city skyline. *Open daily Apr-Sept 10am-7pm, Oct and Mar 10am-6pm, Nov-Feb 10am-4pm. Adm to glasshouses. Inverleith Row, T 0131 552 7171, www.rbge.org.uk*

Edinburgh Zoo ❶ 3C

A modern, spacious zoo set on a hill and home to over a thousand animals. The most famous inhabitants make up the world's largest captive colony of penguins. Each summer afternoon they waddle around the zoo with their keeper in the Penguin Parade. The African Plains experience features walkways spanning the animals' living space. *Open Apr-Sept 10am-6pm, Oct & Mar 9am-5pm, Nov-Mar 9am-4.30pm. Adm. Corstorphine Road, T: 0131 334 9171, www.edinburghzoo.org.uk*

Art Lovers' Edinburgh

Handily for art fans, all of Edinburgh's national galleries (Dean (*see p.13*), SNGMA (*see p.13*), SNPG (*see p.11*), SNG (*see p.10*) and the Scottish Academy (*see p.10*)) share the same opening arrangements and points of contact. They are: **open daily 10am-5pm, Thur 10am-7pm.** Even better, all are free, with charges for some exhibitions. T: 0131 624 2000, www.nationalgalleries.org

Rosslyn Chapel ❹

This incredible example of the art of medieval stone carving – don't miss the famous Apprentice Pillar – lies six miles (10 km) south of Edinburgh (bus 15A). Built in 1466, it's spookily atmospheric. *Open Mon-Sat 9.30am-5pm, Sun 12 noon-4.45pm last adm 30 mins before closing. Adm. Roslin, T: 0131 440 2159, www.rosslyn-chapel.com*

Queensferry ❹

The legendary Forth Rail Bridge and the even larger Forth Road Bridge are engineering marvels on a superlative scale. The rail bridge passes right over South Queensferry, and can be viewed close up from the water too aboard the *Maid of the Forth*, which (in summer) makes an enjoyable outing to monastic Inchcolm Island. On

The Forth Rail Bridge

The great rust-coloured Forth Rail Bridge comprises 54,000 tons of steel, 6.5 million rivets and took seven years to build from 1883-90. At its tallest point, it stands 365 ft (111 m) above the river Forth. There is an exhibition about the bridge at the Queensferry Lodge hotel (open daily) in North Queensferry (❹).

the other side of the bridge at North Queensferry is Deep Sea World, a splendid aquarium (see p.59).

Day Trips

The following destinations are easily accessible by public transport (see p.53) and by car (see p.51).

Dunfermline ❹

Some 30 minutes north of Edinburgh, and once the ancient seat of Scottish kings, Dunfermline today is a relatively quiet little provincial town. Memories of its glorious past are evoked by the

Willow Tea Rooms in Glasgow

atmospheric 13th-century abbey, its ruined medieval royal palace and the 15th-century Abbey House, which is now an award-winning museum. **Tourist info:** *T: 01383 720999, www.visitdunfermline.com*

Glasgow ❸

Edinburgh's vibrant working-class neighbour was a surprising source of erudition even before it became European capital of culture back in 1990. Highlights are the Burrell Collection, the Kelvingrove Museum and the Hunterian Art Gallery. The city's iconic architect and designer, Charles Rennie Mackintosh, is

Stirling Castle

The Apprentice Pillar in Rosslyn Chapel

commemorated at several visitor sites. Regular trains make the 50-minute connection between the two Scottish 'capitals'. **Tourist info:** *T: 0141 204 4400 , www.seeglasgow.com*

Stirling ❸

Gateway to the Highlands. Stirling Castle is reminiscent of Edinburgh Castle (see p.4) in site and layout. It was home to the Scots monarchy until unification under James VI (son of Mary Queen of Scots) in 1603, while William (Braveheart) Wallace is honoured by a spectacular monument visible from the castle. **Tourist info:** *T: 08707 200620, www.visitstirling.org*

edinburgh places to shop

Edinburgh is one of the best cities in Britain, if not Europe, for shopping. It is compact and best of all still very well serviced by the types of interesting individual shops that have been superseded by faceless chain stores in so many other cities. There aren't many major European capitals where you find quirky little shops selling fossils and brooms next to cutting-edge fashion. On top of this, service is nearly always genuinely friendly, interested and personalised. For one-stop shopping there are some good department stores and a handful of modern malls, though you'll find all you need without their help, and have much more fun too!

buy it places to shop

The Royal Mile

Edinburgh's Royal Mile used to be known for its stereotypical tartan and shortbread souvenir shops, but in recent years quality and variety has much improved.

The Fudge House ❷ 5F

The Scots are renowned for their sweet tooth and it's little wonder with temptations like this. Watch the hot fudge being made on a slab in the traditional way. Expensive, but only the best ingredients will do here. *197 Canongate, T: 0131 556 4172, www.fudgehouse.co.uk*

Souvenir shop on The Royal Mile

Geoffrey (Tailor) Highland Crafts

Geoffrey (Tailor) Highland Crafts ❷ 5F

If the kilts are good enough for Sean Connery and Mel Gibson, then Geoffrey can find a suitable one for you. Or perhaps you just want to hire one while you're in town; they do that too. *57-59 High Street, Royal Mile, T: 0131 557 0256, www.geoffreykilts.co.uk.* **Branch:** *Tartan Weaving Mill & Exhibition (see p.19).*

Kinross Cashmere ❷ 5D

Their mills in Loch Leven are where some of the big fashion houses get their their labelled goods woven. Has a good selection of styles and colours all in various weights. Pricey but quality. *2 St Giles Street, Royal Mile T: 0131 226 1577.*

Whisky Galore

There are dozens of different places to buy whisky in Edinburgh and unless you have a particular brand or even style in mind, it's all very confusing. Tastings will help the uninitiated, so look out for these. Shops that have a particularly good selection and knowledgeable staff include Royal Mile Whiskies (*see p.19*), William Cadenhead (also on the Royal Mile) and the wonderful Valvona & Crolla (*see p.24*). Absolute beginners can educate themselves at the Scotch Whisky Heritage Centre at the top of the Royal Mile, which also has a good shop.

Ragamuffin ❷ 5F

Originally from the Isle of Skye your first impression of this gorgeous designer knitwear shop is its high quality Orkney Isles, Shetland and Fair Isle jumpers and cardigans, but there's more here than just traditional Scottish Islands wear with bright contemporary designs from all over the UK and Ireland. Only natural fibres – cotton, wool, silk, linen and merino are used.
278 Canongate, Royal Mile,
T: 0131 557 6007,
www.ragamuffinonline.co.uk

Sweet treats in The Fudge House

Royal Mile Whiskies ❷ 5D

Scotland's largest selection of whiskies, which is saying something. Some date from 1903; all are purveyed by enthusiastic and knowledgeable sales staff who are no strangers to high-level plaudits. Their speciality is single malts though they also carry a huge stock of Irish whiskeys. Scottish beers, Havana cigars and 'herds' of haggis available too.
379 High Street, Royal Mile,
T: 0131 225 3383,
www.royalmilewhiskies.com

Geoffrey (Tailor) Tartan Weaving Mill & Exhibition ❷ 5C

Everything you ever wanted to know about tartan is explained in this working mill. You can even have a go at machine-weaving the cloth yourself. Tartan is on sale by the roll – useful if you want it for making curtains or tablecloths, although bear in mind you will need around eight metres for a full kilt! All manner of tartan and other Scottish memorabilia is on sale. *Castlehill, Royal Mile, T: 0131 226 1555, www.tartanweavingmill.co.uk*

Killer Kilts

If you really want to make a Scottish style statement, and you are feeling bold, head for Geoffrey (Tailor) Highland Crafts to see their 21st-century made-to-order kilts. Silver lizard skin? No problem. Pink plastic see-through? Suits you sir. And check out those contemporary touches like hidden pockets for mobile phones and miniature bottles of mineral water. Click on *www.21stcenturykilts.co.uk* for more ideas and services.

Pine & Old Lace in Victoria Street

Victoria Street & Grassmarket

This picturesque cobbled area is a glimpse into the past, when shops were personal, individual and quirky, rather than soulless corporate clones. Much-photographed brightly painted Victoria Street actually comprises no more than a dozen or so individual shops but taking in the adjacent bohemian Grassmarket too, you can easily spin out half a day or more here.

Armstrong's ❷ 6C

This Bohemian Aladdin's Cave of second-hand clothes specialises in vintage kiltwear and stylish retro gear. So if you're after a 1950s' ballgown, a sharp Zoot suit or the classic Highlander look, this shop will have it. Perfect for parties and themed club nights. *83 Grassmarket, T: 0131 220 5557, www.armstrongsvintage.co.uk*

Fabhatrix ❷ 6C

If you want to keep the Edinburgh wind out of your hair but still look stylish Fabhatrix stock hundreds of individual hats, from dyed wool with matching scarves and wraps, to quirky tweeds with jaunty feathers and hatpins. For balls and weddings or flouncing down George Street, there are retro styles in silk and velvet and Ascot-style 'fascinators'. *13 Cowgatehead, Grassmarket, T: 0131 225 9222, www.fabhatrix.com*

Helios Fountain ❷ 6C

This bright and charming shop is a good place to buy stuff for younger children, with a good range of traditional wooden toys, games and puzzles, cuddly creatures and children's arts and crafts. *7 Grassmarket, T: 0131 229 7884, www.helios-fountain.co.uk*

Iain Mellis Cheesemonger ❷ 6C

If you've ever wondered what Isle of Mull cheddar or Sweet Milk cheese from Morayshire tasted like (nutty with a hint of lemon, actually) drop into Iain Mellis's wonderful smelly shop on Victoria Street and sample before buying. Cheeses come mainly from Scottish farms but you'll find

rounds and wedges from all over Britain and a few from further afield too. Mellis supplies to Edinburgh's best restaurants and has become a byword for top quality. *Closed Sun. 30a Victoria St, T: 0131 226 6215, www.mellischeese.co.uk* **Branches:** *Stockbridge & Bruntsfield.*

Mr Wood's Fossils ❷ 6C
Wonderful quirky little place where, with expert guidance, you can buy

all kinds of fossils, from Scotland and abroad; trilobites, ammonites, dinosaur teeth, fossil fish and plants. *5 Cowgatehead, Grassmarket, T: 0131 220 1344, www.mrwoodsfossils.co.uk*

Pine & Old Lace ❷ 5D
In search of a chemise petticoat, a delicate antique-style duvet, or a set of lace-trimmed bedlinen? How about a pair of Victorian bloomers?

Wonderful cheeses

And with soft golden antique pine bedroom furnishings and fittings to match, no wonder many of the capital's brides-to-be beat a path to this romantic little shop. *Closed Sun. 46 Victoria Street. T: 0131 225 3287.*

Bill Baber ❷ 6C
If you think Scottish knitwear is all unflattering patterns and itchy collars you'll be somewhat surprised by Bill Baber's mini dresses and asymmetrical cardigans. *66 Grassmarket T: 0131 225 3249 www.billbaber.com*

Pretty, brightly painted Victoria Street

New Town

New Town shopping revolves around George Street which is far and away Edinburgh's most elegant and expensive street, dedicated almost exclusively to self pampering, featuring designer clothes and scents and perfumes for him and her. Window shopping here is a treat.

Harvey Nichols ❷ 3E

The gleaming glass place of worship for Edinburgh's fashionistas is surprisingly hospitable for somewhere so swanky. Whatever's hot – from Alexander McQueen to Stella McCartney – is here, so make sure your credit rating is OK, and don't forget to book a table at the Forth Floor (see p.40) for lunch. *30-34 St Andrew's Square, T: 0131 524 8388, www.harveynichols.com*

Neal's Yard Remedies ❷ 3C

Feeling a bit washed out by city life? Try the Covent Garden specialists for their skin and hair care products made from natural ingredients. They also offer a range of complementary medicines, homeopathic remedies, essential oils and herbs. *102 Hanover Street, T: 0131 226 3223, www.nealsyardremedies.co.uk*

Penhaligon's ❷ 5C

This long-established traditional English perfume house sells classic ladies, gents and gender-free scents in countrified shop surroundings. *33 George Street, T: 0131 220 3210, www.penhaligons.co.uk*

Space NK ❷ 5C

This minimalist drop-dead trendy 21st-century apothecary specialises in innovative beauty products from around the world. The name? Well, there is lots of space, and NK are the initials of the company's founder. *97-103 George Street, T: 0131 225 6371, www.spacenk.co.uk*

Glamourous George Street in the New Town

Opening Times

Traditional Edinburgh shop opening hours are Monday to Saturday 9am or 9.30am to 5.30pm or 6pm. On Thursday many shops open late until 7.30pm or 8pm. In recent years Sunday afternoon opening has also become the norm.

Entrance to Harvey Nichols

Princes Street

Dominated by chains, Princes Street is largely forgettable as a shopping location. However it is strong on high-class department stores, with Jenners and Marks & Spencer in the middle and House of Fraser and John Lewis at either end of the street. If you are in town in December, visit the German Market in Princes Street Gardens (*see p.10*), where beautiful traditional handcrafted items are sold.

Edinburgh's oldest department store, Jenners

Jenners ❷ 4D

Edinburgh's grand old lady – founded 1838 – is now looked after by House of Fraser but it her character and charm stays the same. 'The Harrods of the North' is a one-stop high-class Edinburgh gift shop, strong in designer menswear, toys and games, and with the largest lingerie selection in Scotland. Its original oak-panelled galleried Grand Hall is a mini attraction in its own right. *Open daily. 48 Princes Street, T: 0131 225 2442, www.houseoffraser.co.uk*

One World Shop ❷ 4A

A bolt-hole from the crowds, set in the vaults of St John's Church with an exotic selection of crafts, gifts, music and edibles sold under the Fairtrade banner. *St John's Church, Princes Street, T: 0131 229 4541, www.oneworldshop.co.uk*

Waterstones Bookstore ❷ 4B

The chain's biggest branch in Edinburgh is best-known however for its Starbucks Coffee shop featuring wonderful views of the Castle through large bay windows. *128 Princes Street, T: 0131 226 2666, www.waterstones.co.uk*

Museum Shops

Have a look in the National Museum and the National Gallery (*see pp.10, 13*) shops for high-quality gifts, many of which are handcrafted. The Museum of Scotland (*see p.12*) shop is particularly good, with some innovative modern handcrafted items.

Off Princes Street

Fopp ❷4C
The best recorded music shop in Edinburgh with a huge selection of CDs and loads of bargains. They also sell a wide range of music-related items such as books, posters and T-shirts. Helpful staff too. *3-15 Rose Street, T: 0131 243 0870, www.fopp.co.uk*

Just Scottish Gifts & Gallery ❷4C
Tasteful high-quality gifts made by Scottish artists working with ceramics, glass, wood, metal,

Princes Street crowded with shoppers

jewellery and leather. Lovely prints and pictures in the gallery side of the shop. *Open daily. 4-6 North Bank St, The Mound, T: 0131 226 4806.*

McNaughtan's Bookshop ❶2E
The city's best bet for second-hand and antiquarian books, with a large general stock. They will be happy to search out that elusive first edition of Sir Walter Scott for you! *Closed Sun & Mon. 3a-4a Haddington Place, Leith Walk, T: 0131 556 5897, www.mcnaughtansbookshop.com*

Valvona & Crolla ❷2G
Gastronomes, particularly of Italian extraction, will think they have died and gone to heaven on entering this long-established epicurean shrine. Cured meats dangle from the ceiling waiting to be complemented with fresh Italian vegetables, vintage olive oils, fresh sauces, fresh-baked breads and hundreds of other mouth-watering deli lines. Pricey but worth it. Outstanding selection of wines too. You can also taste the goods in the restaurant (see p.47). *19 Elm Row, Leith Walk, T: 0131 556 6066, www.valvonacrolla.co.uk*

Villeneuve Wines ❷2F
This friendly informal independent retailer is one of Edinburgh's largest and most knowledgable wine merchants. *49a Broughton Street, T: 0131 558 8441, www.villeneuvewines.com*

Leith

Georgian Antiques ❶1F
One of the largest selections of antiques in Scotland. A bit out of the way but if you're a serious buyer it's worth the effort. *10 Pattison Street,*

Leith Links, T: 0131 553 7286,
www.georgianantiques.net

Stockbridge

Gramophone Emporium ❷ 1B
Those who have got back into vinyl or never turned their back on it could spend days searching through the rows and rows of 78s. There is a find from all eras for everyone in this shop. *12 & 21 St. Stephen Street, T: 0131 225 1203 www.rare78s.com*

Elaine's Vintage Clothes ❷ 1B
St Stephen Street is excellent for second-hand shopping and this is the best one for ladies clothing. There are some high-quality handmade dresses as well as trinkature and accessories spanning all the fads and fashions of the 20th century. *55 St Stephen Street, T: 0131 225 5783.*

Out of Town

Regular buses *(see p.53)* depart from the city centre to Penicuik and Livingston (❹). Both takearound 30 minutes

Edinburgh Crystal Visitor Centre ❹
Watch Edinburgh crystal-ware being made by expert glasscutters or treat yourself to a classy present – either perfect or seconds. *Adm for tour. Eastfield, Penicuik (bus 15, 15A, 37, 37A). T: 01968 675128, www.edinburgh-crystal.co.uk*

McArthur Glen Designer Outlet ❹
Over 80 discounted designer label and high-street names – Calvin Klein, Reebok, Gap and Armani. Savings of up to 50 per cent. *Almondvale Avenue, Livingston (bus 12, 16, 27, 28), T: 01506 423 600, www.mcarthurglen.com*

Wee dram of whisky in Edinburgh crystal-ware

Top 10 Souvenirs
Take home a Festival Fringe poster from the Fringe Office on the Royal Mile *(see p.33)*; a McSweens haggis (from any good food place); a jokey tartan Tam O'Shanter cap with false ginger hair attached; a stick of Edinburgh Rock; designer woollens and cashmere; a good malt whisky *(see p.18, 19)*; an elegant piece of Edinburgh crystal glass *(see left)*; anything with Jenner's name on it *(see p.23)*; anything tartan *(see p.18)*; chocolate-covered fudge *(see p.18)*.

edinburgh entertainment

Edinburgh is famous the world over for its annual Festival (or Festivals to those in the know) but the city is much more than a two-month wonder. Year round, whatever your predilection — music, theatre, film, comedy, nightclubs — you will be spoiled for choice. The Festival season may only last six or seven weeks but its sense of fun and innovative attitude keeps the city's performing arts scene constantly on its toes. In keeping with the general feel of the city most venues are small- to medium-size, intimate and a pleasure to visit. Sports in Scotland means golf and there are plenty of good courses on the edge of town. Do try another national pastime, rock-climbing, at the Edinburgh International Climbing Arena.

watch it entertainment

Performing Arts

Theatres

Edinburgh Playhouse ❷ 3F

Tastefully restored and seating around 3,000, the Playhouse stages a wide range of popular productions such as West End musical hits *Fosse*, *Fame* and *Miss Saigon*, as well as opera and popular ballets. This is also where you will find the big-name mainstream pop and rock acts (Chris Rea, Blondie). *18-22 Greenside Place,*
Info: *T: 0131 524 3333;*
Bookings: *T: 0844 847 1660,*
www.edinburghplayhouse.org.uk

Edinburgh Playhouse

Traverse Theatre

Edinburgh Festival Theatre ❷ 7E

An impressively grandiose theatre with an imposing glass frontage, the Festival boasts the largest stage in Britain. Major orchestral works are regularly performed here. Look out for contemporary dance and general productions too. *13 Nicholson Street, T: 0131 529 6000, www.eft.co.uk*

Traverse Theatre ❷ 5A

The city's leading venue for cutting-edge and experimental theatre housed in an impressive post-industrial metal-and-glass building, with a bar and a good café. *10 Cambridge St, T: 0131 228 1404, www.traverse.co.uk*

Open-air Theatre

Weather permitting, the Ross Open Air Theatre stages concerts in West Princes Street Gardens all through summer. T: 0131 228 8616.

King's Theatre ❷ 3E

An Edwardian gem which stages just about every kind of mainstream performance art, from Shakespeare to slapstick comedy. *2 Leven St, T: 0131 529 6000, www.eft.co.uk*

Royal Lyceum Theatre ❷ 5A

Fine old Victorian civic theatre, home to Edinburgh's leading mainstream drama production company. *30B Grindlay Street, T: 0131 248 4848, www.lyceum.org.uk*

Usher Hall ❷ 5A

This large rotunda, Edinburgh's finest concert hall, is used mostly for mainstream classical and orchestral performances and pop concerts. *Lothian Road, T: 0131 228 1155, www.usherhall.co.uk*

Comedy Clubs

The Stand ❷ 3E
The top spot for a chuckle, with some of Britain's funniest men and women appearing. Also has a great restaurant and bar. *5 York Place, T: 0131 558 7272, www.thestand.co.uk*

Highlight ❷ 3F
A major player on the Edinburgh comedy scene, this popular comedy chain has the feel of a northern working-men's club. *Unit 6/7, Omni Leisure Development, Greenside Place, T: 0870 787 0707, www.thehighlight.co.uk*

Cinemas

The Cameo Cinema ❷ 7A
Independent, arthouse, cult movies and mainstream blockbusters all get an airing here. *38 Home Street, T: 0871 902 5723, www.picturehouses.co.uk*

Filmhouse ❷ 6A
If you prefer Wim Wenders to Steven Spielberg and you're a sucker for subtitles, this is your kind of place. *88 Lothian Road, T: 0131 228 2688, www.filmhousecinema.com*

Pop & Rock

HMV Picture House ❷ 5A
Converted art deco cinema with atmospheric auditorium and bar areas. Established Indie and Dance acts back in up to 1500 punters. *31 Lothian Road T: 0844 847 1740, www.hmvtickets.com*

Cabaret Voltaire ❷ 6E
The atmospheric bar-cum-nightclub attracts up and coming bands from across the country as well as local talent. Live music events every night, and acts range from rock bands to live DJs. *36 Blair Street, T: 0131 220 6176, www.thecabaretvoltaire.com*

The Corn Exchange ❶ 4C
The best venue in town for seeing big-name popular bands, just the right size – big enough to accommodate around 2,000 punters but not so huge as to be totally impersonal. *11 New Market Road, T: 0131 477 3500, www.ece.uk.com*

The Liquid Room ❷ 5D
An excellent venue, usually frequented by local R&B and indie bands but often playing host to famous groups too. It also doubles up as a very popular nightclub. *9 Victoria Street, T: 0131 225 2564, www.liquidroom.com*

Queens Hall ❶ 3E
This lovely converted church seats up to 800 and hosts an eclectic range of performers, from mainstream rock to world, folk, jazz and eclectic classical music concerts. *85-89 Clerk Street, T: 0131 668 2019, www.thequeenshall.net*

Whistle Binkies ❷ 6E
Sweaty cellar bar just off the Royal

Rocking it at the Liquid Room

Mile where local rock, pop, blues and occasional folk bands bang out covers and their own stuff to a young raucous crowd, Wed-Sun until 3am. Open mic Monday, open bands Tuesday. Adm charge after midnight Friday and Saturday. *4-6 South Bridge, T: 0131 557 5114, www.whistlebinkies.com*

Jazz

The Jazz Bar ❷6E
Voted 2010 UK Jazz venue of the Year. Gigs and jam sessions seven days a week. Expect a varied programme – including blues, soul, funk and acoustic – alongside some emerging and established jazz artists. *1A Chambers Street, T: 0131 220 4298, www.thejazzbar.co.uk*

80 Queen Street ❷3C
Live jazz three nights a week, guest bands on Fridays; house band on Saturday with their stomping arrangements of old favourites. Free admission. Music starts 9pm. *80 Queen Street, T: 0131 226 5097, www.eighty-queen-street.com*

Folk Music

Folk music is very popular in Edinburgh. The best venues are:

Sandy Bell's ❷7D
Seven nights of music plus Saturday and Sunday afternoons. *25 Forrest Road, T: 0131 225 2751.*

Royal Oak ❷6E
Sessions every night. *1 Infirmary Street, T: 0131 557 2976, www.royal-oak-folk.com*

Edinburgh Folk Club, The Pleasance Cabaret Bar ❷7F
Music on Wednesday nights at 8pm. Tickets only on sale at the door. *60 The Pleasance, T: 0131 650 2458, www.edinburghfolkclub.co.uk*

The Ensign Ewart ❷5D
Folk music on Sunday nights and often more live music on Tuesday and Thursday nights as well. *512 Lawnmarket, Royal Mile, T: 0131 225 7440.*

Ceilidh @The Lot ❷6C
Come and ceilidh (pronounced

Reel the night away ...

'caley') at the Caley ('cally'!) on a Tuesday night. This is a traditional Celtic evening of music and dance with a caller and band led by a fiddle player. Learn to reel and dance the Strip the Willow – it's fun and also great exercise! *4-6 Grassmarket, T: 0131 225 9922, www.the-lot.co.uk*

Clubs

The Bongo Club ❷6G
An established eclectic club that has just moved venue and where the music varies nightly. *37 Holyrood Road, T: 0131 558 7604, www.thebongoclub.co.uk*

Citrus Club ❷5A
Saturday nights boast the best indie

music in the city, with other themed nights a regular occurrence. The dungeon-like feel simply adds to the mystique. *40-42 Grindlay Street, T: 0131 622 7086, www.citrusclub.co.uk*

City ❷ 5E

Part of a complex that includes a sports bar and swanky restaurant, the club varies between chart, party, classics and house. *1a Market Street, North Bridge, T: 0131 226 9560, www.city people.info*

Sneaky Pete's ❷ 6D

Dark and intimate club with small stage that attracts an open-minded music loving crowd. Club nights and gigs showcase experimental Indie, Electronica and Hip-Hop acts and DJs. *73 Cowgate, T: 0131 225 1757, www.sneakypetes.co.uk*

Opal Lounge ❷ 5C

A trendy nightspot that should be sampled at least once. Superb decor and sounds, and an impressive cocktail menu. *51a George Street, T: 0131 226 2275, www.opallounge.co.uk*

Po Na Na ❷ 3C

A favourite with the George Street set who enjoy funk, disco, R&B, hip hop, salsa (lessons provided), house and chart. A different theme nightly. *43B Frederick Street, T: 0131 226 2224.*

Shanghai ❷ 5C

You'll find some of the trendiest revellers in the city here. Great for a lavish night out. *16 George Street, T: 0131 270 3914, www.shanghaiclub.co.uk*

Festival Time

August in Edinburgh is partytime. The International and Fringe festivals get top billing but the **International Film Festival**, the **International**

Logo at the entrance to City

Book Festival (both last two weeks August) and the **International Jazz & Blues Festival** (ten days starting in late July) are major events in their own right. Click on www.edinburghfestivals.co.uk for details of this year's events.

The Edinburgh International Festival

The Edinburgh International Festival, started in 1947, is the more formal mainstream part of the Edinburgh Festival, staging over 150 productions of opera, dance, theatre and classical music, many of world-class standing, from mid August through early September. Although the performances spread right through the city (*see p.28 for venues*) the centre of all the activity is The Hub near the Castle, where there is a café, ticket shop and various performance spaces. On the final Saturday of the International Festival a magnificent firework display erupts from the castle ramparts, lighting up the whole city. *The Hub, Castlehill, T: 0131 473 2001, www.eif.co.uk*

Marching in time at the Military Tattoo

The Edinburgh Military Tattoo

The most famous event of the festival, however, is the Edinburgh Tattoo, a spectacular military show and parade staged nightly on the esplanade of the Castle, watched live by 220,000 people annually and televised worldwide. With its unique blend of music, ceremony, entertainment and theatre set against the amazing backdrop of Edinburgh Castle, it is one of the world's greatest shows. *32 Market Street, T: 0131 225 1188, www.edintattoo.co.uk*

The Edinburgh Fringe Festival

The world's largest arts festival sees over 15,000 performances, squeezed into three weeks, shoe-horned into every conceivable nook and cranny of the city. The majority of productions are small scale theatre, but every genre of the performing arts is represented. Big names do appear, often in homage to the fact

Performers on parade in the Fringe

Entertaining the crowds...

they made it at the Fringe in years gone by, but the vast majority of performers are young unknown hopefuls. The content and quality ranges from the ridiculous to the sublime, always pushing the limits, often outraging public decency, but also throwing up tomorrow's top mainstream performers too, particularly in the field of comedy. The annual Edinburgh Comedy Awards, established in 1981, rewards The Best Comedy Show, Panel Winner and Newcomer – and often leads to TV deals and commercial success. *180 High Street, T: 0131 226 0026, www.edfringe.com*

Sports & Activities

Edinburgh International Climbing Arena ❶ 5A

This amazing cavernous space, an old quarry with a roof on top, is the biggest rock-climbing centre ever built, which opened in 2003 and immediately hosting the World Cup Indoor Climbing Finals. Three artificial rock faces ascend to 60 feet (30 m)

Acrobatics at the Fringe

Ways of Making the Most of the Fringe

- Go to The Mound every-day for a great free show by buskers – do drop some money in the hat – and free previews of acts as a taster for the shows that evening.
- Pick up the local papers in the morning and look for special offers on tickets for that day. You may have to collect tickets in person.
- Read the reviews to eliminate some of the turkeys. But if something turns out to be complete nonsense, it's part of the Fringe experience.
- Don't overdose and try to see too many shows.

and replicate climbing conditions from beginners to international level. At the very top is the dizzying SkyRide aerial ropeway course. No previous experience, just a sense of adventure required! *South Platt Hill, Ratho (10 miles (16 km) west of city centre, off A71), T: 0131 333 6333, www.eica-ratho.com*

Golf

The Scots are passionate about golf and there are good municipal pay as-you-play courses a bus ride away at Braid Hills (*T: 0131 447 6666*) and

The climbing wall at the Climbing Arena

Craigmillar Park (*T: 0131 667 0047*). Just out of town at Musselburgh (**④**) is a good nine-hole links course that claims to be the oldest in the world and costs around £12: *T: 0131 665 5438*. If you are a keen golfer and you have a car, it's worth travelling further to the courses below. Beware – they are expensive! *www.scotlands-golf-courses.com*

Gullane Golf Club ④
Pronounced 'Gillin', and around 20 miles (32 km) east of town, you can choose from three links courses with panoramic views. *West Links Road, Gullane, T: 01620 842 255, www.gullanegolfclub.com*

Muirfield (The Honourable Company of Edinburgh Golfers)
This famous championship course hosted the British Open in 2002. A handicap is required to play; men 18, ladies 24. *T: 01620 842 123.*

North Berwick Golf Club
A championship links course with far-reaching views. *Beach Road, North Berwick, T: 01620 892135.*

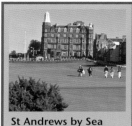

St Andrews by Sea
Any golfer worth his salt will want to play at the mecca of the St Andrews Old Course some 40 miles (65 km) north of Edinburgh (and accessible by train from Edinburgh to Leuchars) but it is down to luck whether you get a tee. Applicants are entered into a daily ballot so your chances depend on how many people want to play that day. If you can't get on the course, then there's the consolation of saving the green fees and also ten other courses to choose from. *www.standrews.org.uk*

Horse Racing

Musselburgh race course, six miles (10 km) east of Edinburgh, is one of the best small courses in Britain and is the busiest in Scotland. There is a regular year-round programme of quality steeplechasing and flat racing. *See the local paper for details, or T: 0131 665 2859, www.musselburgh-racecourse.co.uk*

Ice Skating

In December a temporary ice rink is created in Princes Street Gardens right next to the Scott Monument (*see p.11*) so you can skate to classical music under the stars – and directly below the great looming bulk of the castle rock.

Skiing

Midlothian Ski Centre ❶7E
Europe's longest dryslope, at 400 metres, gives space to practice skiing and snowboard techniques under expert tuition. *Biggar Road, Hillend, T: 0131 445 4433, www.midlothian.gov.uk*

Swimming

Leith Waterworld (❶2F) has lanes for serious swimmers, flumes for the kids and a learner lagoon and sloping 'beach' pool for water babies. *377 Easter Road, Leith, T: 0131 555 6000, www.edinburghleisure.co.uk*

Spectator Sports
Football

There is little love lost between the two Edinburgh teams, Hibernian (Hibs, ❶2F) and Heart of Midlothian (Hearts, ❶3D). There is a home

Sledging on the nursery slope at Hillend

match most weekends in the season. *www.hibs.co.uk, www.heartsfc.co.uk*

Rugby

Murrayfield (❶3C) is home to the Scottish national rugby team and there is a great atmosphere in the city on match days. *T: 0131 346 5000, www.sru.org.uk*

Cricket

Scotland's various representative teams can be seen competing against English counties and Test playing stars at The Grange (❶2D). *Raeburn Place, T: 0131 332 2148, www.thegrangeclub.com*

What's On, Where
Buy a copy of *The List* for comprehensive listings of all events (film, music, theatre, comedy, gay, clubs, art, kids and sport) in Edinburgh. The paper comes out fortnightly on a Thursday (*see p.61*).

edinburgh places to eat

Not so long ago Edinburgh boasted some very good traditional pubs, a handful of high-quality traditional restaurants and a small number of cheap bohemian eating places living mostly off the Festival. The pubs, thankfully, are still there but over the last decade the eating and drinking scene has mushroomed and now matches, if not exceeds, most European capitals in quality, quantity and variety. From Michelin-starred Modern Scottish chefs to simple, stylish cafés on almost every street corner, from fashionistas at the designer bars of George Street to the pub-crawl boozers of Rose Street, the city really does offer drinking and dining for every budget and every conceivable taste.

taste it places to eat

Scottish

Café Royal Oyster Bar £££ ❷ 4E

Possibly Edinburgh's most famous eating venue, the Café Royal is divided into various rooms each offering its own drinking and eating experience. The 140-year-old Oyster Bar is a sumptuous Victorian time warp with fish and game delicacies that Boswell would still recognise and enjoy. *17A West Register Street. Open daily lunch & dinner.*
T: 0131 556 4124,
www.caferoyal.org.uk

Doric Tavern £ ❷ 5E

Close to the train station this pub has an atmospheric dining room upstairs that's all creaky floorboards, fast service and an interestingly mixed clientele (especially during the festival). The menu offers simple gourmet pub stuff at very decent prices – their Sunday Roasts (12-5pm) are a fine way to spend the day of rest. *Open daily lunch and dinner. 15/16 Market street,*
T: 0131 225 1084, www.the-doric.com

Dubh Prais £££ ❷ 5E

Dubh Paris (pronounced doo prash) understated grandeur makes for a fine but not overly pricey dinner, with wood panelling, starchy white tablecloths and staff that appear and disappear just when you want them to. Serving all manner of beasts that have fed on Scottish grass or swam in its seas, there really is no better place to sample the finest game, salmon, beef and lamb.
Open Tue-Sat dinner only. 123b High Street, T: 0131 557 5732,
www.dubhpraisrestaurant.com

Forth Floor, Harvey Nichols ££-£££ ❷ 3E

A gastro scene isn't a gastro scene without a Harvey Nichols nosherie. Perfect for trendsetters who lunch, and those on a mission to impress. *Open Mon lunch only, Tue-Sat lunch*

Contemporary Caledonian Cooking

The days when Scottish cooking meant deep-fried Mars Bars and cheap artery-clogging stodge are almost a distant memory. Modern Scottish cuisine takes the very best local, often organic produce, such as Aberdeen Angus beef, native venison, raspberries and local cheeses, and then adds ingredients from around the world and a contemporary touch to provide delicious and unusual dishes such as beef with shiitake mushrooms and malt whisky cream, venison with vanilla and shallot jus, and even crispy haggis spring rolls with sweet chilli sauce!

& dinner. 30-34 St Andrew's Square,
T: 0131 524 8350,
www.harveynichols.com

Howies £-££ ❷ 3D

'No fuss, no faff', but that doesn't

stop Howies turning out top-quality Modern Scottish dishes at very reasonable prices and in time to allow you a full day's sightseeing too. The Provence-style branch at Victoria Street is particularly appealing. Also branches at Waterloo Street, Bruntsfield and Stockbridge. All branches BYOB. *Open daily lunch & dinner. 10-14 Victoria Street, T: 0131 225 1721, www.howies.uk.com*

Oloroso £££ ❷ 4B

This restaurant offers probably the most unusual and innovative Modern Scottish menus in town with Oriental and Eastern influences. The views – the Forth to one side, the castle to the other – are spectacular.

Contemporary-styled game dish

Outside the Café Royal

Open daily lunch & dinner; bar 11am-1am. 33 Castle Street, T: 0131 226 7614, www.oloroso.co.uk

The Tower ££-£££ ❷ 5D

Vanessa Redgrave eats here when in town. Wonderful views over the Castle and superlative service. *Open daily 12 noon-11pm. Museum of Scotland, Chambers Street, T: 0131 225 3003, www.tower-restaurant.com*

The Witchery by the Castle £££ ❷ 5C

The Witchery is acclaimed as one of Scotland's finest eating places mixing contemporary local food with Gallic and international influences. The setting, a 16th-century merchant's

Meals with a View

Combine sightseeing with dining: here's a few of the best restaurant views in Edinburgh. Forth Floor, Harvey Nichols (*see p.40 & pic*); Heights at the Apex International Hotel in the Grassmarket (❷5C); The Tower (*see left*); Oloroso (*see p.40*); the Starbucks at Waterstone's (*see p.23*); Pizza Express, Stockbridge, with its terrace overlooking the Water of Leith (❶2D); The Place to Eat, John Lewis (*see p.23*).

house is very atmospheric, particularly its downstairs Secret Garden, which is Edinburgh's most romantic venue. Its pre/post theatre menu is a bargain. *Open daily lunch & dinner. Castlehill, Royal Mile, T: 0131 225 5613, www.thewitchery.com*

Seafood

L'Alba D'Oro £ ❷ 1C
You can't visit Edinburgh without sampling its fried fare. This New Town chippy (fish and chip shop), near the Botanic Garden, serves fish, squid, prawns, even mushrooms in the lightest batter alongside properly cooked golden chips all wrapped up in yesterdays Evening News. If you're offered "sass" it means a brown sauce/vinegar combo. *Open daily 5-11pm. Henderson Row, T: 0131-557 2580, www.lalbadoro.com*

Fishers Bistro ££ ❶ 1F
A busty mermaid figurehead welcomes you to this friendly cosy

little wine-bar style restaurant which has a great reputation for serving some of the best and most inventive fish and seafood dishes in Leith. *Open daily 12 noon-10.30pm, bar later. 1 The Shore, Leith, T: 0131 554 5666.*

Mussel Inn ££ ❷ 4C
If you're hankering for seafood at a sensible price in Edinburgh the bustling Mussel Inn, owned and run by shellfish farmers, is unbeatable. The emphasis is on mussels, scallops and oysters, and huge portions of moules 'n' chips in various sauces – are great value. *Open Mon-Sat 12 noon-10pm, Sun 1.30pm-10pm. 61-65 Rose Street, T: 0843 2892 481, www.mussel-inn.com*

Shore Bar & Restaurant ££ ❶ 1F
Half traditional pub and half cosy though formal white-linen dining room, the Shore is a Leith institution where top-quality fish and shellfish, albeit at a price, can be enjoyed in very convivial surroundings. *Open daily lunch & dinner. 3-4 The Shore, Leith, T: 0131 553 5080.*

French

Le Café St Honoré ££ ❷ 3C
Picturesque romantic Café St Honoré

Proper Pubs
Despite the rapid march of modernisation and a rash of style bars shooting up in recent years, Edinburgh still retains many fine old pubs (*see box, p.42*). Their time-worn wood, glass and decorative tile fittings are masterpieces of Victorian and Edwardian design. Most pubs open all day, and the standard closing time is 11pm, but at weekends and during summer they often stay open until 1am.

serves typical high-class Parisian brasserie meals with *je-ne-sais quoi élan*. Come early (6pm-7pm) for their set-price specials at £13.50 for two courses and a bargain £18 for three courses. *Open Mon-Sat lunch & dinner. 34 North West Thistle Street,* T: 0131 226 2211, www.cafesthonore.com

Petit Paris ££ ❷ 6C

The checked table-cloths, French staff and accordion music will kid you into believing you are in Paris rather than the Grassmarket. The

Classic Moules

menu includes authenticities such as *cocotte* (stew) and *saucissces de Toulouse*. They even hold fondue and *moule* parties! *38-40 Grassmarket,*

Stylish interior of The Kitchin

A Pint o' Heavy and a Wee Nip, Please

If you want to try the local beer in Edinburgh, ask for a pint of 'heavy'. It's similar to traditional English Bitter though generally sweeter tasting. You will normally be served an '80 shillings' (80/-), which is what the tax was on a barrel in days gone by, and so is an indicator of alcoholic strength. There may also be a 70/- brew available. Whisky comes in larger nips or drams (measures) than in England and the small metal tap on the bar is for you to add water, if you wish. Single malts are smoother than blends brands and are somewhat more expensive.

T: 0131 226 2424,
www.petitparis-restaurant.co.uk

The Kitchin £££ ❶ 1F

Tom Kitchin – one of Edinburgh, nay the UK's most celebrated chefs

Your Good Pub Guide

The small, snug Jolly Judge, Lawnmarket (❷3A), off the Royal Mile; The Kenilworth and The Abbotsford (❷4D), two traditional Rose Street drinking dens; Bennet's Bar, Leven Street (❶3E); the Barony Bar, the Cask & Barrel and Mathers Bar (❷2F), all on Broughton Street; the Oxford Bar, Young Street (❷3B), where Detective Rebus drinks (see p.61); the Cafe Royal Circle Bar (see p.39) with its glorious tiles. Well worth the walk is the Sheep Heid Inn at Duddingston (see itinerary), a village inn with decent food and a lovely outdoor patio.

– slept on Paris floors to learn his trade. Edinburgh's all the better for his return with this chic but cheerful restaurant that serves sumptuous, inventive dishes. Bookings essential. *Open Tue-Sat for lunch and dinner. 78 Commercial Quay, T: 0131 555 1755, www.thekitchin.com*

Bistros & Brasseries

Hadrian's Brasserie ££ ❷4E

Located in the Balmoral Hotel, Hadrian's elegant lime walls and silky service will soothe the most shopped out shopper or refresh even the worst case of festival fatigue.

Tempting Mediterranean fare

The Balmoral, 1 Princes Street, T: 0131 557 5000, www.hadriansbrasserie.com

indigo (yard) £ ❶3D

Fashionable but friendly joint. Dishes – Italian, Oriental, Mediterranean and local produce – are creative and filling. *Open daily for food 8.30am-10pm. Bar open daily until 1am. 7 Charlotte Lane, T: 0131 220 5603, www.indigoyardedinburgh.co.uk*

Maxies Bistro and Wine Bar £-££ ❷5D

Maxies is justly renowned for its splendid location. This Edinburgh institution nestles on a gorgeous terrace that, weather permitting, can elevate a simple summer meal to whole new heights of loveliness. The inside is very pleasant as well, and the menu will delight vegetarians and fans of seafood in particular. The wine list is well worth getting to know. *Open daily 12 noon-11pm. 5b Johnston Terrace, T: 0131 226 7770.*

North Bridge Brasserie ££ ❷5E

Dramatic contemporary-classical

splendour on a split level, featuring marble pillars, dark wood, glistening mirrors and a splendid oval central bar area in the former reception hall of *The Scotsman* newspaper office building. Delicious food, with affordable dishes too, and perfect for a romantic night out. *Open daily lunch & dinner. 20 North Bridge, T: 0131 622 2900, www.northbridgebrasserie.com*

Wildfire Bistro £ ❷ 4B

The word is obviously out about this informal and affordable bistro which is a-buzz with dinners tucking into big steaks and stringy fries.
192 Rose Street, T: 0131 225 3636, www.wildfirerestaurant.co.uk

Cafés

27. The Restaurant ££ ❷ 4A

An elegant restaurant and simple but stylish coffee shop, housed in one of the city's most lovingly restored Georgian buildings (*see p.11*), also home to the Scottish National Trust. Despite this both are refreshingly unstuffy. The restaurant (lunch only)

serves the best of Scottish produce with enough contemporary style to keep all parties happy. *Open Mon-Sat 12 noon-4pm. 28 Charlotte Square, T: 0131 243 9339.*

Café Hub £ ❷ 5C

Beautifully laid out in an old church a few steps from the castle, the Hub is a firm favourite with locals (the International Festival offices are based here, *see p.32*) and visitors. Cappuccino and cake as well as top-quality brasserie food at reasonable prices with occasional culinary events. In summer book a table on the terrace overlooking The Royal Mile. *Open 9.30am-6pm daily. Castlehill, Royal Mile, T: 0131 473 2067, www.thehub-edinburgh.com*

Café St. Giles £ ❷ 5D

An Edinburgh institution. March up the stairs and take a window seat with views over Princes Street Gardens. Once a pioneer of continental café style, now it has a somewhat faded Bohemian charm. Their Belgian waffle with syrup and cream is the stuff of legends!

Café Hub interior

Open Mon-Sat 9am-5pm, Sun 11am-5pm. 8 St Giles Street, T: 0131 225 5147.

City Art Centre £ ❷ 5E

This bright cheerful space with huge murals is as popular with Mums and children as arty types visiting the adjacent gallery. The food – quiches, toasties, baked potatoes etc. – is simple but well done. *Open Mon-Sat 9am-5pm, Sun 12-5pm. City Art Centre, 1-2 Market Street, T: 0131 220 3359, www.edinburghmuseums.org.uk*

Grand Designs on George Street

A number of grand capacious century-old former banking and financial institutions on George Street (❷ 3B-3D) have been converted to become some of Edinburgh's most truly spectacular drinking and dining spaces; All Bar One, Standing Order, Tiles, Grape and the extraordinary Dome Bar & Grill. Visit the latter to stare at its eponymous Cathedral-like ceiling. The food here is highly rated, too.

Breakfast Parisian style

The Elephant House £ ❷ 6D

A legendary Edinburgh establishment where students and literati gather at communal tables in the atmospheric backroom to linger over coffee and gaze over Greyfriars Kirkyard (see p.12). Good salads and snacks by day, more substantial dishes in the evenings – if you can find a space to eat them. *Open daily 8am-11pm. 21 George IV Bridge, T: 0131 220 5355, www.elephanthouse.biz*

The Queen Street Café £ ❷ 3E

Fancy a coffee with Sean Connery? Well, at least his portrait by John Bettany, which is one of several splendid artworks adorning the National Portrait Gallery's (currently closed but will reopen in Autumn 2011) dark brick refreshment rooms. Good soups and salads and scrumptious home-baked cakes. *Open Mon-Sat 10am-4.30pm, Sun 11am-4.30pm. Scottish National Portrait Gallery, 2 Queen Street, T: 0131 557 2844.*

Vegetarian

Cornerstone Café £ ❷ 4A

Tucked beneath St John's Church (see p.23) at the west end of Princes Street, the Cornerstone

(the best-kept secret in town!) is a perfect peaceful bolthole from the crowds and shops. Bag a battered sofa and chill out beneath the cool stone vaulted ceiling. It's toothsome veggie meals and tasty snacks all the way. *Open Mon-Sat 9.30am-4.30pm. Lothian Road, T: 0131 229 0212.*

David Bann's Vegetarian Restaurant & Bar ££ ❷ 6F

Vegetarian food has never looked classier than at David Bann's. It's not cheap but the worldwide array of flavours, the inventive dishes and the attractive dining room make it very worthwhile. *Open daily for lunch and dinner. 56-58 St Mary's Street, T: 0131 556 5888, www.davidbann.com*

Henderson's Restuarant £ ❷ 3C

The old-fashioned interior could do with a spruce up but the food is as good as ever at Edinburgh's original vegetarian café-restaurant and just one look at the mouthwatering counter display should convert even the most diehard carnivores. Live

music most evenings and BYOB are two more good reasons to visit. Just round the corner is the recently refurbished bistro. *Open Mon-Sat 8am-10pm, and Sun 10am-4pm in Aug and Dec only. 94 Hanover Street, T: 0131 225 2131, www.hendersonsofedinburgh.co.uk*

Delicious vegetarian fare

Around the World

California Coffee Company Kiosks £

The California Coffee Company has painted the old Edinburgh police boxes red and turned them into coffee franchises. Good quaffing and good times.

It's Kids' Stuff

With its range of brasseries and excellent cafés offering snacks and mains at the same table, Edinburgh is easy on families. Other places particularly good for children include Brown's (❷ 3B) on George Street, Henderson's Restaurant (*see left*), Pizza Express, Stockbridge (❶ 2D), and the Wild West-themed branches of the Buffalo Grill at Chapel Street (❶ 3E), and Raeburn Place, Stockbridge (❶ 2D). Teens love Hard Rock Café on George Street (❷ 3D).

Cool Cocktail Bars

To the west of George Street lie some of Edinburgh's trendiest designer bars. Startting at Bar 38 (*126 George Street,* **②** *3B*), head east towards Tiger Lily and Lulu downstairs (*125 George St,* **②** *3B*), Oloroso (*33 Castle Street,* **③** *2B*), Rick's (*55a Frederick Street,* **②** *3C*) and the Dome (**②** *3D*) Elsewhere trendy young Edinburghers frequent Bar Missoni (*King George IV Bridge,* **②** *5D*), Dragon Fly (*Grasmarket,* **②** *6B*) and in Leith, The Bond (**①** *1F*).

Hanedan £ **②** 4E

It's a bit out of the way (it's just beyond the Queen's Hall) but this small but bright and buzzing Turkish restaurant is so worth the effort. Everything is creamed, marinated or chargrilled to perfection by the chef, owner and youngish Turk, Gursel Bahar. *Open Tue-Sun for lunch and dinner. 41 West Preston Street, T: 0131 667 4242, www.hanedan.co.uk*

Kalpna ££ **①** 3E

Long regarded as the best Indian vegetarian restaurant in the city, Kalpna specialises in the cuisine of the Gujarat region. Great value. *Open Mon-Sat. 2 St Patrick Square, T: 0131 667 9890, www.kalpnarestaurant.com*

Lancers Brasserie ££ **①** 2E

The colonial days of the Raj are recalled at this famous restaurant which has been patronised by Billy Connolly, Elton John and other megastars. Fortunately the food lives up to the billing. The gingery chicken murgh in particular is wonderful. *Open daily lunch & dinner. 5 Hamilton Place, Stockbridge, T: 0131 332 3444, www.lancersbrasserie.co.uk*

Maison Bleue £-££ **②** 5D

A little bit of what you fancy is the principle here, and gorgeous mouthfuls of French, Vietnamese, Moroccan and Scottish dishes (consumed tapas-style) make

Traditional pad thai

it easy to be principled. With its stone arches, deep blue walls and rustic sofas Maison Bleue has a relaxed Mediterranean feel. Interesting and good value. *Open daily lunch & dinner. 36-38 Victoria Street, T: 0131 226 1900.*

Thai Orchid ££ ❷ 5C

A huge golden Buddha, plinky plinky music and traditionally dressed maidens – and maidmen – greet you at this popular Thai restaurant. Everything tastes fresh and flavoursome and is beautifully presented. The business lunch has a limited number of classics but is fabulous value. *Open daily for lunch and dinner. 5a Johnson Terrace, T: 0131 225 6633, www.thaiorchid.uk.com*

Valvona & Crolla £-££ ❷ 2G

It's almost impossible not to feel hungry walking through the V&C shop (*see p.24*) so it makes perfect sense to put some of their wonderful ingredients to immediate use. The café-restaurant set under a beamed pitched roof has an almost Alpine

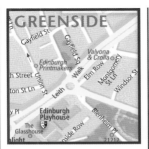

feel and the food is Italian gourmet home-cooking, although local produce also gets a look in. Try the sizeable *antipasti* platter for a taster of many items on sale in the shop. It's not cheap but you can BYOB (as long as you buy your bottle in the shop!) with a £4.00 corkage charge. *Open daily. 19 Elm Row, Leith Walk, T: 0131 556 6066, www.valvonacrolla.co.uk*

Vin Caffé ££ ❷ 3E

This sister restaurant of Valvolla & Crolla is right nextdoor to Harvey Nicks. It serves really great coffees,

panini and drinks downstairs whilst upstairs, the swanky dining room – complete with its own film projector – serves authentic classic Italian dishes and the wines that other Italians seem to want to keep to themselves. *Open Mon to Sat lunch and dinner, Sun for lunch. 11 Multrees Walk, T: 0131 557 0088, www.valvonacrolla.co.uk*

Haggis 'n' Neeps

It may be better not to know but the traditional Scottish national dish, haggis, is the chopped up heart, liver and lungs of a sheep cooked with oatmeal and onions inside its stomach bag. It is always accompanied by 'tatties (mashed potatoes) 'n' neeps' – what the Scots call turnips, and what the English call swede. Tatties 'n' neeps combined are also known as 'clapshot'. Have a wee dram of whisky as accompaniment – it works very well.

edinburgh practical information

As European capital cities go Edinburgh is very small – its centre is comparable to Amsterdam or Dublin – so finding your way around is very easy. The city is built on a number of steep hills, and if you should occasionally not feel like walking to wherever you want to go, then public transport will get you there quickly and cheaply. The bus services are efficient, there are taxis to be hired and there's never any need to be a martyr to weary legs. There's little to concern or confuse you (except maybe the weather, which at best is unpredictable and at the worst downright awful) plus almost without exception, the good folks of Edinburgh are cheery and friendly. And from here there are day trips to be had to Glasgow, the Borders and the Highlands.

know it practical information

Tourist Information

VisitScotland ❷ 4E, ❹
Open winter daily Mon-Sat 9am-5pm, Sun 10am-4pm. Summer open daily 10am-6pm.

Branches:
Waverley Station: *Princes Mall, Princes Street;* **Edinburgh Airport.** *Both can make accommodation bookings. T: 0845 225 5121, www.visitscotland.com.*

Old Town Information Centre ❷ 5E
Tron Church, Royal Mile, open daily summer 10am-5.30pm, winter 12 noon-5pm.

Arriving by Air

Edinburgh Airport (❹) is eight miles (12 km) west of the city. It handles domestic and international scheduled flights plus transatlantic charters. *T: 0844 481 8989, www.edinburghairport.com*

Arriving by Train

East Coast
Provides the east coast of mainland Britain with a fast, efficient service to and from London King's Cross to Edinburgh Waverly Station taking around 4 hours. **Customer service:** *T: 08457 225 333, www.eastcoast.co.uk*

Virgin Trains
Runs from London Euston ro Edinburgh Waverly various routes change at Birmingham, the total journey itime is 4.5 to 6 hours. **Enquiries:** *T: 08719 774 222, www.virgintrains.co.uk*

Scotrail
Provides a Scotland wide service and the Caledonian Sleeper service to and from London (overnight, takes 7-8 hours). Glasgow to Edinburgh is 50mins. **Enquiries:** *T: 0845 601 5929, www.scotrail.co.uk*

To check out cheap tickets visit the train operators own websites or *www.thetrainline.com.* All train information is also available through

Edinburgh Airport sign

National Rail Enquiries, *T: 08457 484 950.*

Getting into Town
From the Airport

An **Airlink bus** (No. 100) is run by Lothian Buses (*T: 0131 555 6363*) between the airport and city centre; it takes around 25 minutes, departs every 10 minutes and terminates by Waverley Bridge (❷ 4E) outside the railway station. Buy tickets at the booth by the bus stop or on board

(£3.50 one way, £6.00 return).
www.flybybus.com

Taxis cost about £20 to Princes Street.

From the Train Station

Waverley Station (**2** 4E), at the east end of Princes Street, is as about central as you can get. From Haymarket (**1** 3D) to the west end of Princes Street is a 10-minute walk, or catch bus no. 3, 3A, 12 or 25.

Banks

Most banks open Monday-Friday 9am/9.30am-4pm, and sometimes staying open until 5.30pm. Many also open Saturday mornings.

Changing Money

The main options are the hotels, post offices, banks, exchange bureaux (in the tourist office (*see p.50*), at Thomas Cook branches) and ATMs, which are found outside most banks. Shop around for the best deals if you are changing large amounts and only use your hotel as a last resort.

Local Currency

The unit of currency is the pound (£) sterling, divided into 100 pence. The notes and some coins have different designs to the English ones but they are legal tender throughout the UK.

Bike & Car Hire

Bicycles

Only recommended for experienced urban cyclists! The centre of town in extremely hilly. Good places to cycle are: in and around Holyrood Park (*see p.8*), along the Water of Leith Walkway (**1** 6A-5C); and near Stockbridge (**1** 2E), where an old railway line has been converted to a flat cycle route. **Spokes**, a local pro-cycle action group, publish a map of the city's cycleways; *www.spokes.org.uk*

Edinburgh Cycle Hire

Hire a bike from £10 and £15 per day or £50 to £70 per week.
www.cyclescotland.co.uk

Car Hire

Hire a car for trips out of town. In town they are a liability as parking space is pricey and restricted. Few hotels have parking, wardens are strict and clamping is commonplace.

Avis (Terminal Building, airport)
T: 0844 544 6004, www.avis.co.uk

Alamo (Terminal Building, airport)
T: 0870 191 6921, www.alamo.com

Hertz (Terminal Building, airport)
T: 0870 846 0009, www.hertz.com

Trains at Waverley station

Climate

Edinburgh is a cool northern city and even in high summer, temperatures rarely rise much above 20 degrees C. August is ususally warm, but it can also be wet; the best months to visit are May and June. In winter the east wind blows and the mercury plummets to near zero. It rains all year round and proximity to the coast and hills means the weather is changeable throughout the day, so be prepared for all eventualities! The locals say that if you don't like the weather then wait 20 minutes.

A bus stops on Princes Street

Disabled Access

All new buildings in Edinburgh are wheelchair-friendly, but the Old Town (*see p.4-6*) has cobbles, steep stepped alleyways and attractions housed in medieval buildings. **Tourism for All**, *www.tourismforall.org.uk*, and the **Disabled Persons Transport Advisory Committee** website, *www.dptac.independent.gov.uk*, are good resources for disabled travellers. In addition, **Visit Scotland** can advise you as to the accessibility of accommodation, sites and streets in Edinburgh, *T: 0845 22 55 121.*

Emergencies

For all emergency services: *T: 999.*

Internet Cafés

easyinternetcafe ❷ 4B
Open daily 7.30am-10.30pm. 58 Rose Street, www.easyinternetcafe.com

Edinburgh Internet Café ❷ 6C
98 West Bow, www.edininternetcafe.com

E-Corner Internet Cafe ❷ 6E
55 Blackfriars Street, www.e-corner.co.uk

Left Luggage

There is an attended left-luggage Bus Station office in Waverley Station (❷ 4E) on Platform 1 and self-service lockers in St Andrew's Square (❷ 3D), a couple of minutes walk across Princes Street.

Personal Safety

In general Edinburgh is a very safe city, but it is as well to know it does have significant drugs problems in certain suburbs. Take the usual big-city precautions and don't venture through the narrow alleyways of the Old Town (*see p.4-6*) or across The Meadows fields (❶ 3E) late at night.

Pharmacies

The pharmacy with the longest regular opening hours is Boots. For a listing of late-opening pharmacies (usually until 10pm) see local papers.

Boots ❷ 4A

Open Mon-Fri 8am-8pm, Sat 8am-6pm, Sun 10.30am-4.30pm. 46-48 Shandwick Place, T: 0131 225 6757.

Post Offices

St James Shopping Centre ❷ 3E

Edinburgh's main post office. Open Mon, Wed-Fri 9am-6pm, Sat & Tue 8.30am-6pm, east end of Princes Street, T: 0845 722 3344 .

Normal post office hours are Monday-Friday 9am-5.30pm and Saturday 8.30am-12.30 or 1pm. Local branches may close for lunch and close one afternoon in the week. A postcard to the USA costs 56p.

Public phone box

Public Holidays

These differ from the rest of the UK.

1 Jan	*New Year's Day*
2 Jan	*New Year's Holiday*
March/April	*Good Friday*
March/Apri	*Easter Monday*
April	*Spring Holiday*
1st Mon May	*May Day*
3rd Mon May	*Victoria Day*
Nearest Sat to	
1st July	*Trades Holiday*
1st Mon Aug	*Bank Holiday*
September	*Autumn Holiday*
25 December	*Christmas Day*
26 December	*Boxing Day*

Public Phones

Most public telephones only accept phone cards, although some take cash and others accept credit cards. Phone cards are available from newsagents and some supermarkets in denominations of £2.00 upwards. Please be aware when buying that these only work on phones owned by the individual card company.

Local and national newspapers

International Codes

Australia: *T: 61*, **Canada:** *T: 1*,
Irish Republic: *T: 353*,
New Zealand: *T: 64*, **USA:** *T: 1*.
To call Scotland from abroad:
T: 0044.
All numbers in the city have the prefix *0131*.

Public Transport
On the Buses

The biggest operator in Edinburgh is **Lothian Buses** (*T: 0131 555 6363, www.lothianbuses.com*) whose purple-liveried vehicles usually provide a frequent and punctual service. Lothian fares are £1.10 for a single ticket. Do bear in mind that you'll need the exact fare across the city given. **Daysaver** tickets (offering unlimited use) cost £3.00 for a standard ticket. Night buses run half-hourly through the night across the city centre. Pick up the very useful mini-size leaflet, *Edinburgh's Frequent Bus Map*, from the tourist office (*see p.50*).

Taking a Taxi

Taxis comes in two types; traditional (mostly) black cabs, which may be hailed in the street and work on the meter, and mini-cabs, which can only be called by phone – the drivers will negotiate their own fares with you according to destination. Always agree the fare before you get in a mini-cab. As a rule of thumb, black cabs are cheaper in town (unless you are stuck in traffic!), but mini-cabs may be a better deal for longer rides. Never get in a mini-cab if the driver is touting for trade on the street. If you're happy with the service, a tip of around 10 per cent is the norm.

Sightseeing
Opening Times

All Edinburgh's national art galleries share the same opening times (*see box, p.14*). Most other museums open Monday-Saturday from 10am-5pm and also Sunday afternoons during at least July and August. Private attractions tend to have longer opening hours and most open on Sunday all year. During the Festival season (*see pp.32-33*) in August and September, all venues tend to open for an hour or two later in the evening.

Sightseeing Passes

If you are considering visiting more than a couple of Historic Scotland attractions (which include Edinburgh Castle (*see p.4*), Stirling Castle (*see p.15*), Linlithgow Palace (**4**) and, in the Borders, Jedburgh Abbey), it's worth investigating an Explorer Pas. £22 for 3 days, £31.50 for 7 days. T: 0131 668 8600, www.historic-scotland.gov.uk

Tipping

Scotland is not a very tip-conscious society. However, if service is good, tip restaurant waiters and taxi drivers around 10 per cent (*see left*), porters around £1.00 per bag, chambermaids £1.00–2.00 per night.

Tours
Walking Tours

The highly entertaining **McEwans 80/- Literary Pub Tour** is a great way to learn about the city's literary history. You also to get meet people, and see the pubs at the same time. It meets at 7.30pm daily from June to September at the Beehive Inn,

Edinburgh taxi

Grassmarket (**❷ 6C**). Just turn up. For other times of year, call for details on *T: 0131 226 6665, www.scot-lit-tour.co.uk*

If it's a fright you're after, you can't beat the **City of the Dead** tours (*see box, p.6*) but there are a dozen or so other spine-tingling walks that take you through the backstreets and sometimes deep underground in the alleyways and built-over tenements of the Old Town. These tours are advertised on billboards by the Mercat Cross (**❷ 5D**) and at the tourist information office (*see p.50*). For a conventional but entertaining and insightful walking tour of the Royal Mile, try **Mercat Tours**, which also meet daily by the Mercat Cross. Ring for times and details: *T: 0131 225 5445, www.mercattours.com*

Open-top Bus Tours

There are four operators (Britannia, City, Edinburgh and Mac Tours), who all offer similar tours of the city and depart regularly daily

Spooky Mercat Tours

from Waverley Bridge (**❷ 4E**), by the station (*see p.50*). To help you choose the most suitable for your requirements – hop-on hop-off or whole-city tour, multi-lingual or single language, best route, prices and so on – click on *www.edinburghtour.com*

Coach Excursions

Day trips run as far north as Loch Ness and the Highlands, but it's

better to stick to low-mileage excursions such as to St Andrews (*see box, p.34*) or the Borders. If you prefer a more personal touch to the standard coach tour, try **Rabbie's Trail Burners** (*T: 0131 226 3133, www.rabbies.com*), who use 16-seater mini-coaches. Pick up details of other tours at the tourist office (*see p.50*).

Open-top Mac Tours bus

directory

Whether you are a regular visitor to Edinburgh or a first-timer, this section will help you to get the most out of the city, from finding the best hotels to suit your budget to discovering some small but equally fascinating visitor attractions that were not included in earlier chapters. There are ideas for entertaining young families, from exploring aquariums to using Victorian cameras, plus details of annual events, ideas for further reading and useful websites. There is even a 'language' section to help you along with the local dialect – have a braw day!

Key to Icons		Price Guide
Hotels		**Per double room**
Room Service	@ Business Centre	£ Under £50
Restaurant	Health Centre	££ £50-£100
Fully Licensed Bar	❄ Air Conditioning	£££ £100-£150
En Suite Bathroom	P Parking	££££ £150-£250
		£££££ Over £250

Places to Stay

Edinburgh has a good choice of accommodation for all budgets and should be able to fit you in most of the year. August, which is Festival time, however requires booking a long way ahead to get your first choice, and this is when prices soar through the roof. The tourist office (see p.50) will book accommodation for you for a £4.00 charge. Many people let their houses and apartments out during the festival; look in local papers and at the Festival offices (see pp.32-33) for further information.

Posh Traditional

The Balmoral £££££ ❷ 4E

An Edinburgh landmark and as central as it gets, the five-star Balmoral is the choice of visiting heads of state and rock stars. Rooms have every conceivable luxury and wonderful views. *1 Princes Street, T: 0131 556 2414, www.thebalmoralhotel.com*

Roxburghe Hotel £££ 3E

One of Edinburgh's real traditional old haunts, with classically furnished rooms and subtle public areas. It has an enviable position on the corner of the Georgian marvel that is Charlotte Square (see p.11).
38 Charlotte Square,
T: 0131 225 1251,
www.edinburghintercontinental.com

The Scotsman Hotel £££££ 5E

This superb, five-star rated conversion of the former Scotsman (Edinburgh's leading local news sheet) editorial office is now a city institution. All the original features, such as the marble staircase and walnut-panelled lobby, have been preserved and oh-so-stylish bedrooms and suites have been added. There's a brasserie (see p.42) and restaurant, health club and spa and fabulous stainless steel pool.
20 North Bridge,
T: 0131 556 5565,
www.thescotsmanhotel.co.uk

Posh Cool

The Bonham ££££ 3D

A very clever blend of 19th- and 20th-century styling behind a grand Victorian townhouse facade, voted one of 'the world's coolest hotels' by Condé Nast Traveller magazine. All 48 rooms retain period features but are equipped with all the latest electronic toys and decorated with works by up-and-coming Scots modern artists. 35 Drumsheugh Gardens, T: 0131 226 6050, www.thebonham.com

The Glasshouse £££££ 3F

Edinburgh's most ambitious boutique hotel. The striking entrance is through a mid-19th-century brick church façade into an airy lobby of marble granite and glass. All 65 rooms and suites, full of high-tech wizardry and modern art works, enjoy views from the city or towards Calton Hill. The peaceful rooftop garden is a wonderful retreat for an early-evening aperitive.
2 Greenside Place, T: 0131 525 8200,
www.theetoncollection.com

Hotel Missoni ££££ 5D

Those who find bright colours and angles interrupt their sleep might want to give it a miss. But for those who love modernity and clever design, the Missoni is the ultimate Edinburgh hotel. The bar and restaurant, Cucina, are so good, you won't want to leave but, most charmingly, the thoughtful extras thrown make you feel genuinely pampered rather than like they're squeezing every last penny out of you. 1 George IV Bridge, Edinburgh EH 1AD, T: 0131 220 6666, www.hotelmissoni.com

Malmaison £££-££££ 1F

Located in a gorgeous old waterside building which was once a seaman's mission, the extremely stylish Malmaison offers affordable chic in trendy Leith. Parisian Art Nouveau

touches flourish in the brasserie.
Tower Place, Leith, T: 0131 468 5000,
www.malmaison.com

Point Hotel £££-££££ ❷6A

Central Edinburgh's most
reasonably priced chic boutique
hotel, featuring multi-award winning
contemporary interior minimalist
design, converted from an old
department store. It includes a
very popular highly rated bar and
restaurant. Some of its 140 rooms
enjoy castle views. *34 Bread Street,*
T: 0131 221 5555,
www.pointhoteledinburgh.co.uk

The Rutland £££ ❷4A

This historic Edinburgh Townhouse
has had an oh-so stunning refit,
bringing together handsome original
features with gorgeous colours and
fittings. Its bar, genuinely good
restaurant and luxe cocktail bar –
The One Below – feel more like NYC
than Edinburgh: it's only the burr
of the staff's voices and the haggis

and porridge served for breakfast
that tells you otherwise. *1-3 Rutland*
Street, T: 0131 229 3402,
www.therutlandhotel.com

History & Romance

The Witchery Suites £££££ ❷5C

A very atmospheric 16th-century
stone building next to Edinburgh
Castle (*see p.4*) has 11 outlandishly
luxurious suites, fitted and furnished
in theatrical ultra-romantic Gothic
or Baroque style, replete with
antiques, drapes, tapestries and
other authentic fixtures. all of which
ingeniously conceal the mod cons.
This is frequently ranked among
the world's most romantic hotels
and there is an equally romantic
restaurant (*see p.39*). *Castlehill,*
Royal Mile, T: 0131 668 3346,
www.thewitchery.com

Prestonfield House £££££ ❶4F

Nestling below Arthur's Seat, just a
few minutes walk from Princes Street,
Prestonfield is surrounded by 20

acres of parkland and has the feel of
a country estate. Suavely refurbished
by James Thomson, owner of The
Witchery (*see left*) and The Tower
Restaurant (*see p.39*), this 17th-century
mansion now offers 30 rooms in
eclectic and opulent style complete
with state-of-the-art 21st-century
gadgetry as well as public areas filled
with fine art and antique furnishings.
Priestfield Road, T: 0131 225 7800,
www.prestonfield.com

Affordable

Apex Waterloo Place £££ ❷4F

Just up the stairs and round the
corner from Waverly train station, it
offers superb value for money which
means the money conscious needn't
skimp on quality or style. A king
sized bed, soft fluffed up bedding,
flat screen TV, newspapers, free
WiFi and a little rubber duck to take
home all come as standard whilst
a breakfast fit for a king will see
you on your way. Check for deals.
27 Waterloo Place, T: 0131 523 1819,
www.apexhotels.co.uk

Ten Hill Place £££ ❷ 7E

Close to the Festival Theatre, this hotel is technically a 3 star but you'd never know it. Large, bright rooms with big beds and spotless bathrooms (although the glass doors on these may panic some). Breakfasts are bountiful and the staff eager to keep everyone happy. *10 Hill Place, T: 0131 662 2080, www.tenhillplace.com*

University of Edinburgh Pollock Halls £££ ❶ 4F

Edinburgh University rents out accommodation all-year round in various townhouses and halls nearby the bucolic Holyrood Park (*see p.8*). Salisbury Green, Kenneth Mackenzie and Masson House all have excellent rooms at a price that suits the budget traveller. *18 Holyrood Park Road, T: 0131 651 2007, www.edinburghfirst.com*

Kids' Venues

Brass Rubbing Centre ❷ 5E

Housed in a peaceful retreat off the Royal Mile, in one of Edinburgh's oldest churches, and with a very interesting history which Mum and Dad will appreciate. *Open Apr-Set Mon-Sat 10am-4.30pm; closed for lunch 12-1pm. Last rubbing at 3.45pm. Trinity Apse, Chalmers Close, T: 0131 556 4364, www.edinburghmuseums.org.uk*

Camera Obscura ❷ 5C

The ancient art of large-scale pinhole camera technology, though all youngsters need understand is that they can magically see right down on to Princes Street as if they were looking through a huge telescope. Save it for a clear day and 'scoop' people up as they walk across the road in front of the building. Holograms and other illusion techniques provide a good belly-laugh for all ages in rooms off the winding stairs. *Open daily Apr-Oct 9.30am-6pm (later in July, Aug), Nov-Mar 10am-5pm. Adm. Castlehill, Royal Mile, T: 0131 226 3709, www.camera-obscura.co.uk*

Deep Sea World ❹

A state-of-the-art aquarium featuring one of the world's longest underwater tunnels, where sharks and rays swim within inches of your head. North of the city centre in North Queensferry; combine with a visit to the awesome Forth road and rail bridges (*see p.14*). *Open Nov-Mar Mon-Fri 11am-5pm, Sat-Sun 10am-6pm. Apr-Oct & school holidays daily 10am-6pm. Adm. T: 01383 411 880, www.deepseaworld.com*

Don't Forget:

Edinburgh Zoo (*see p.14*), the whimsical **Museum of Childhood** (*see p.6*), and best of all, **Our Dynamic Earth** (*see p.8*), which should not be missed. Kids also love the colour and excitement of the International Festival and the antics of the Fringe; they have their very own festival in late May (*see p.60*).

Annual Events

For information about all of Edinburgh's festivals and events visit *www.edinburghfestivals.co.uk*

25 January

Burns' Night: A celebration of the Scottish poet involving serenading a haggis by the bagpipes, consumption of whisky (*see box, p.41*) and the recital of Burns' poetry.

Mid-April

Edinburgh International Science Festival: Huge city-wide programme of innovative and entertaining events for all ages, with lots of hands-on activities, based on science and technology. *T: 0131 558 7666, www.sciencefestival.co.uk*

1st May

Beltane Fire Festival: Paint your face with blue woad, put on your best New Age gear and celebrate the arrival of spring with various fiery pagan-like goings-on up at the top of Calton Hill (*see p.8*). *www.beltane.org*

June

Edinburgh Marathon (❶1F): This well-established gruelling event takes place in the middle weekend of the month. The marathon follows a picturesque route around the Old Town and Castle, along Princes Street through the north of the city and along the shoreline to Leith before returning to Holyrood Park. *www.edinburgh-marathon.com*

Late May-early June

International Children's Theatre Festival: Britain's biggest performing arts festival for children (age three to 12 as a rough guide) with 10 days of children's theatrical and musical events, including magic shows, puppetry, mime, poetry, book readings and so on. *www.imaginate.org.uk*

Third week June

Royal Highland Show (❹): The highlight of the country calendar with a vast cornucopia of Scottish food, pedigree livestock, flower show, craft fair, show jumping and many other agricultural and rural pursuits over four days. Ingliston, near Edinburgh airport, *T: 0131 335 6200, www.royalhighlandshow.org*

Last fortnight in June

Edinburgh International Film Festival: 12 days of premieres and special viewings, attracting big names and big audiences. *T: 0131 228 2051, www.edfilmfest.org.uk*

August-September

Edinburgh International Festival (*www.eif.co.uk*), **Edinburgh International Book Festival** (*www.edbookfest.co.uk*) **and Fringe Festival** (*www.edfringe.com*): A two-month period of cultural invasion involving media from all over the world. Hotel and rental rates soar upwards, as do restaurant prices, and half of the city is at a standstill (*see pp.32-33*).

Late November-Christmas Eve

Edinburgh's Christmas: Three weeks of festive events centering around Princes Gardens, which acquires a giant ferris wheel, a funfair, an ice rink, a German Market and other traditional Christmas craft

and market stalls (*see p.10*).
www.edinburghschristmas.com

Late December-1 January
Hogmanay: Four days of intense partying in the streets of the capital, including a torchlight procession, fantastic fireworks over the Castle (*see p.4*) and big-name bands bring in the New Year. Tickets go on sale in July. *T: 0844 894 2011,* www.edinburghshogmanay.com

Further Reading

Scratch below the surface; there is more to Edinburgh literary life than Sir Walter Scott.

The Strange Case of Dr Jekyll and Mr Hyde, **Robert Louis Stevenson**. Based on life in the 19th-century Old Town.

The Prime of Miss Jean Brodie, **Muriel Spark**. Middle-class mores of the mid-20th century, set in the posh suburb of Morningtonside.

Trainspotting, **Irvine Welsh**. Lowlife and the violent subculture of drug abuse, set in Leith in the 1990s.

Knots and Crosses, Hide and Seek, The Hanging Garden, **Ian Rankin**. Just three of the many popular Detective Inspector Rebus novels exposing the sordid underbelly of contemporary Edinburgh.

Complicity, The Bridge, **Iain Banks**. Two crime thrillers set in Edinburgh by another best-selling modern writer.

Newspapers

The Edinburgh Evening News and *The Scotsman* are two Edinburgh-based daily newspapers. On Sundays *Scotland on Sunday* is published by the same company. There are also regional editions of the main English papers. International newspapers are on sale at various city-centre newsagents. The **International Newsagent** (*351 High Street, Royal Mile*) has a wide selection of European and US papers.

Listings Magazines

The List (on sale fortnightly) is the definitive guide to what's on (*see box, p.35*). Also the *Edinburgh Metro* is daily in the week and free.

Websites

www.edinburgharchitecture.co.uk
Discover the secrets of the Old Town (*see pp.4-6*).
www.scottish.parliament.uk
Have your political say and monitor the progress of this infamous building (*see box, p.8*).
www.weddinginedinburgh.com
Should you wish it, everything you need for the perfect nuptials.
edinburghnews.scotsman.com
International and local news.
www.edinburghguide.com
Comprehensive and easy-to-use listings guide to what's on.
www.edinburgh.org
Round-up of all the local attractions from the Lothians Tourist Board.
www.timeout.com/edinburgh
Good old reliable all-rounder with lots of detail and refreshing outlook.

speak it

Scottish is a dialect of the English language. The Edinburgh accent is soft and more easily comprehensible to visitors than accents in other parts of Scotland. Here are a few terms that you may encounter on your trip to the city:

auld – old.

The Auld Alliance – historic link between Scotland and France.

The Auld Enemy – possible reference to historic enmity between Scotland and England.

Auld Reekie – literally Old Smokie, an archaic nickname for Edinburgh, referring to the days when raw sewage ran from the Old Town into the Nor' Loch (see box, p.10).

awa' wi' ye' – go away (polite form!).

bonnie – pretty, beautiful.

braw – fine, good (often used of pleasant weather).

burn – a stream.

ceilidh – a gathering of people together for Gaelic music-making, singing and dancing (pronounced 'caley', see box, p.31).

clan – family or Highland tribe (for example the MacDonald clan).

close – small courtyard (many in the Old Town, for example Mary King's Close (see p.5).

couthy – nice, pleasant.

douce – mild, gentle, kind (also used of good weather).

dram – a small slug of alcohol, normally whisky (see box, p.41).

dreich – dull, wet, miserable, of weather (pronounced 'dreech', with a guttural 'ch').

glen – a Highland valley bordered by hills.

haggis – often believed to be a small Highland animal. In fact a tasty dish served with 'neeps' (see box, p.47).

heavy – beer (see box, p.41).

ken – know (as in **d'ye ken**...?/ do you know.....?).

Irn Bru – a fizzy soda drink rarely seen south of the border.

kirk – a church.

laird – a landowner.

lassie – a young girl.

loch – lake (as in Loch Ness).

nip – a measure of whisky (see box, p.41).

Sassenach – non-Scots person (usually pejorative, of English people) and occasionally used to refer to people from the lowlands.

see you! – hey! (to attract attention; be careful with this as it can be perceived as aggressive).

Slainte! – cheers! (pronounced 'slange').

wee – small.

wynd – narrow alleyway between houses.

ye' no' too bad – you're OK (term of mild approval!).

info@popoutmaps.com
www.popoutproducts.co.uk

Written by Paul Murphy.
Updated by Shona Main.
All Pictures © Compass Maps
Ltd, Edinburgh Smith & Steven
Douglas except 3, 49 V. K.
Guy ltd; 4L, 9R, 10L, 11L, 12R,
13R, 14L, 15M, 21R, 24L, 25M,
27, 33L&R, 39L, 41M, 42M,
44M, 45, 46L&R, 51, 53, & 54
Shutterstock; 10R, 29L, & 50
iStockphoto; 17 Nick Dryhurst/
PCL; 18L Martin Third; 30 Rob
Wilson; 37 Alamy; 34R Glyn
Satterley/VisitScotland; 39R
www.rampantscotland.com
Cover Images: Chad Ehlers/
Tips Images & Fintastique/
iStockphoto.

Whilst every effort has
been made to trace the
photography copyright
holders, we apologise in
advance for any omissions.
We would be pleased to insert
appropriate credits in any
future editions.

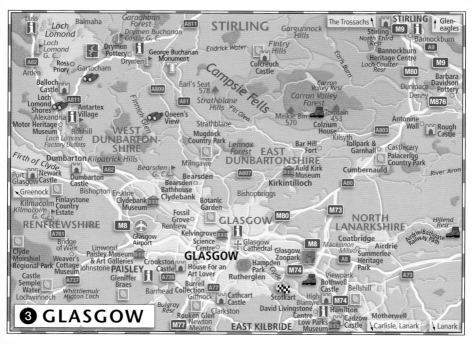

③ GLASGOW